# Book of Diamonds

Church of Diamonds

Cadmus Publishing
www.cadmuspublishing.com

Copyright © 2022 Church of Diamonds

Cover art by:

Published by Cadmus Publishing
www.cadmuspublishing.com
Port Angeles, WA

ISBN: 978-1-63751-296-8

All rights reserved. Copyright under Berne Copyright Convention, Universal Copyright Convention, and Pan-American Copyright Convention. No part of this book may be reproduced, stored in a retrieval system, or transmitted in any form, or by any means, electronic, mechanical, photocopying, recording or otherwise, without prior permission of the author.

# Table of Contents

Acknowledgements ................................................................. 1

Kabili Prayers ........................................................................ 3

Book of Diamonds ................................................................. 9

Prophets of Principles .......................................................... 49

## Acknowledgements

The Church of Diamonds would like to pay homage to the people that's considered family, that help make this happen. It took a very particular set of energies, spirits and personalities to help form this scripture. Principles and attitudes of the likeminded men and women formed the foundation of the Church of Diamonds. For this we want to take some time out to honor them:

To the mother that took on the task of being the glue, we thank you.

To Lil Goonie B, we acknowledge your growth and sacrifice, we thank you for that.

To Goonie Mack, we acknowledge your Integrity that helped to make this happen, we thank you.

To Blue Note, we acknowledge your transformation and dedication, we thank you.

To Red Dollas, we acknowledge your ambition and your willingness to face adversity, we thank you.

To Lil Rollie, we acknowledge your loyalty and your willingness to learn, we thank you.

To Blue Chipz, we acknowledge your generosity and metamorphosis into a divine being, we thank you.

To Chucky, we acknowledge your love and the willingness you give it with, we thank you.

To Blue Dollaz, we acknowledge your wisdom and commitment, we thank you.

To Elsa, we acknowledge your trustworthiness and your faith, we thank you.

# CHURCH OF DIAMONDS

# Kabili Prayers

CHURCH OF DIAMONDS

## Kabili Prayer #1

Before I die Kabili, embrace me with your love.
Bless me with the gifts that only you can provide.
Guide me to the truth and steer me away from the lies.
Give me the perfect balance between ego and pride.
Kabili keep me grounded in my morals and values.
Bless away the imperfections of a treacherous coward.
At my lowest show me that my imperfections is power.
I'ma product of ya strength so within is power.

## Kabili Prayer #2

What's love without passion? Hearts are the manifestation of compassion. Been through war trials but never committed war crimes. Violations of the universal laws that govern the thoroughbreds have never been under siege more than now hence war trials without war crimes shall be the motto. Walk the earth on all ten, never have to pay a fine. Equanimity in the face of opposition. He can get it fine. Jewel choosing for material, not for myself but to spread the wealth. Each one, teach one, you uplift we all rise. If you only look to destroy then your cause of all our demise. Be perspicacious, warrior-like, and wise.

# BOOK OF DIAMONDS

# CHURCH OF DIAMONDS

# Book of Diamonds

CHURCH OF DIAMONDS

## COMMANDMENTS

1. Thou shall not kill without provocation
2. Thou shall not rape
3. Thou shall not molest
4. Thou shall not betray Fellow Diamonds
5. Thou shall not slander without merit
6. Thou shall not condemn one to slavery or assist one in slavery
7. Thou shall not commit child murder
8. Thou shall not do drugs that are not from the earth unless for medical reasons
9. Thou shall be disciplined in all actions.
10. Thou shall remain humble in all dealings with all

## Penances for Violation of Commandments

A 7 day fast

A cleanse of the body for 30 days (No drug substances or alcohol)

A blood sacrifice under the instruction of the Senior Diamond

Diet

No processed food. Everything that is consumed by the body rather meat or fruit shall be organic. Do not defile the temple.

## Chapter 1: Book of Diamonds

Kabili is the energy that permeates through us all. Kabili is the culture that energizes the masses. Kabili is the essence of the oppressed. Kabili is never surrendering and utterly resilient. Kabili is the energy that resides within good and evil. Kabili is the unknown. Kabili is the ineffable. Kabili is what all seek but few find. Kabili is the love without hate and the hate without love. The ultimate oxymoron. Kabili is never judgmental but always skeptical Kabili is the most hated by the masses because Kabili is the mirror of their hypocrisy. Kabili is most misunderstood by those that don't understand themselves. Kabili is the reality without perception. Kabili is the absence of conscious and more of the subconscious that dominates the conscious. Kabili is the ruler of minds. Kabili is the heart of valiant man. Kabili is defiant in the face of a tyrant. Kabili is the one who stands trial rather than betray a loved one. Kabili is the one that rather live on his feet, than die on his knees. Kabili is rebellion. Kabili is the faculty of a sound mind. Kabili is the revenge inside of vengeance. Kabili is the justice that is sought without fear of reprisals. Kabili is the retaliation for the slain. Kabili will not balk at blood but is the farthest from being bloodthirsty. Kabili is the curse on the treacherous. Kabili is the laughter at the vainglorious. Kabili is the glory of a victory. Kabili is the legs of a victor. Kabili is the weight that builds strength. Kabili is battle born and tested. Kabili is the concrete that has endured. Kabili is the tears of a mother who has endured labor. Kabili is the unloved. Kabili is the manifestations of the oppressed population. Kabili is the foster child raised in foster homes. Kabili is the aborted baby. Kabili is the lost man seeking death to be found. Kabili is the unwanted. Kabili is the one that has been thrown away, under the guise of being beyond redemption, but Kabili is redemption. Kabili is the residue of abandonment. Kabili is the soul of the fallen. Kabili is the integrity that stands its ground under the threats of penalty of sentence. Kabili is the one that cannot be led astray but rather the one that leads others. Kabili is the one that scrutinizes others including self. Kabili is the one that never seeks conflicts but never withdraws from it. Kabili is the one that never rattles in the midst of chaos. Kabili is solitary while remaining social. Kabili is the eyes of the focused. Kabili is the protector of the unprotected Kabili is substance without material hence can never be corrupted by material. Kabili is eternal, never swayed by ephemeral possessors. Kabili is the guiding light out of self-destruction. Kabili is the understanding that blossoms out the impoverished communities. Kabili is the ocean of sins and the cleanser of evils. Kabili is the crowd energy that pulsates throughout the people. Kabili is the allure of murder, the intrigue of mystery. Kabili is the pressure that makes diamonds. Kabili is the obstinacy that is the result of being the most hated. Kabili is never bitter, knowing that all is temporary including emotions. Kabili is all of us within the culture. Kabili is the culture. The spirit of the underdog comes from the culture of the oppressed. The spirit that is manifested out of this oppression is Kabili. Now Kabili has come to be our support system in defiance of our oppressors, there to give us guidance on our principles, morals, and values. Now we have a scripture to the spirit that we've felt the whole time. A guide to our way of life. Words that we've felt and spoken in our communities for decades are now in a book of worship. Just for us. There is no need for conjectures anymore, the answers are here. The answers to problems and questions that are unique to us and our daily struggles. Our society has deemed us wrong and unjust but this could not be farther from the truth. Our culture ensures that we adhere to a code of conduct that is different than that of societies, and for that we have been relegated to the bottom of the caste system. Kabili is here to tell you (among many other things) that just because you have a different belief system does not mean that you are inferior. You are of the soil. Your thoughts are just as natural as the soil because they are a product of that soil. Never be ashamed to flaunt your lifestyle or what you represent. Our boldness is what makes our culture so contagious. Almost everything in pop culture is a direct descendent of us. So be ashamed of what? Of being authentic? You are diamond cut. Rejoice in that. Rejoice in the fact that you stand on your own two and never look to hold others responsible for your decisions. Responsibility is that quality of a diamond. People who criticize us look to delegate blame and call it just. How is this so? This is the refusal to accept responsibility. A follower of

Kabili must stand firm on responsibility. Every action causes a reaction, this is karmic energy. This is where responsibility for your actions come into play. Stand firm on the blessings or repercussions that are a direct descendent of your actions without looking for anyone else to thank or blame. You are strong enough to endure responsibility. Responsibility is a reflection of strength of character. Contrary to belief, justice is not a shift of responsibility to someone else. Vengeance a natural human feeling that we do not have to put into code words, or feel ashamed for feeling. Justice is subjective though not objective, the universe did not give us this individual feeling to burden others with. We are not to delegate our sense of justice to others to deal with for us. This is an individual feeling that should be an individual choice to deal with as you like as long as it does not impede on non-involved parties liberty. It is very important when dealing with the karmic energy not to impede on the liberty of people who have not offended. Seek justice individually, however that may look for you but do not seek justice from the ultimate hypocrisy of state sanctioned entities. This is forbidden. This is not natural. In our purest form there is no organized unit that seeks justice, only individuals. What can be more pure than uncorrupted individual justice? A Sense of justice that has not been corrupted by a hypocritical societal view. Justice is what you perceive it to be, not what others tell you it is. Be wary of those with the answers.

## Chapter 2: Responsibility

---

A man must stand on principle. Kabili has blessed us with the energy to do so. Not to do so would be counterproductive to the abilities that have been given to you and a violation of commandment number nine to remain disciplined. The scripture is meant to embolden the future steps of a believer. To provide guidance and wisdom. Not to confuse and lead one into hypocrisy or submission. Submission is for the weak and the pliant. Kabili is neither. Kabili works cohesively with the believers, giving energy that is palpable and easily tapped into. Energy that makes it easy to stand on ones morals, values, and integrity. To have principles is an easy thing but to stand on them is always an arduous task. There is temptation around every corner but diamonds are made under pressure and revel in the challenge that the temptations sets. There will be tests. A Lot of the time people will be this test, and just like a test you must pass on these people.

Others parade around in masks looking to fool you, the disciplined recognizes the fool with the mask and distances oneself from that fool knowing that only foolishness can come from the association. One has to be perspicacious to identify the treacherous qualities in a fool. This is not an easy thing to do, keeping in mind that some actors are better than others. But even the best of actors slips in their facades.

  A tell-tale sign of what's to come and that's when your reason must trump emotion and you must withdraw. If a snake hisses don't stand still and wait for the bite. Now you are the fool. Not only a fool but a bitten fool. The possibility of death is ever present so to allow yourself to be bitten could be a lesson that you never get the chance to learn from. If you are bitten, never blame the snake for doing what's in its nature. Never look to play victim. You are the embodiment of Kabili and Kabili is no victim. Looking for outside sources to blame for your lack of cognizance is a cop out. One must take responsibility for his/her actions or lack thereof. If you put yourself in position to be bitten you are the blame not the snake. Surely there were signs of human scales but somewhere in your dealings with this person you neglected to give them any credence. Shame on you, but there is time for redemption if the bite wasn't fatal and that is utilizing the wisdom that you paid so dearly for. History is littered with those that did not learn from history. We can have all the knowledge in the world but if it is not put to use it is useless. IF you have a friend and you know this friend to be promiscuous and to have a history of sleeping with past friends significant others and you bring your significant other around this friend, having this knowledge, and they have sex with each other behind your back, who is to blame? Surely not your friend that has scales. Don't fall victim to playing the victim. You are to blame. You knew this friend history of being promiscuous and sleeping around with others mates but you disregarded that knowledge and brought your mate around anyway. Surely you knew this was a possibility. You had the knowledge and the wisdom that this person was a snake/fool yet you still allowed yourself to be bitten by not steering clear of this snake, in open field. Kabili has given you the wisdom and the knowledge to see the snake but you cursed that blessing by not utilizing these attributes you were given. The snake will not be reprimanded for being a snake no more than you will be reprimanded for not paying heed to the signs. Remember that people will only do what you allow. Be cognizant of who you allow in your life because with them comes the energy that they bring that will ultimately affect your energy. Their energy should be conducive to yours. Kabili radiates positivity. To allow negative energies around you only leads to negative things happening to you or around you. Remember positivity is a choice.

## Chapter 3: Generosity

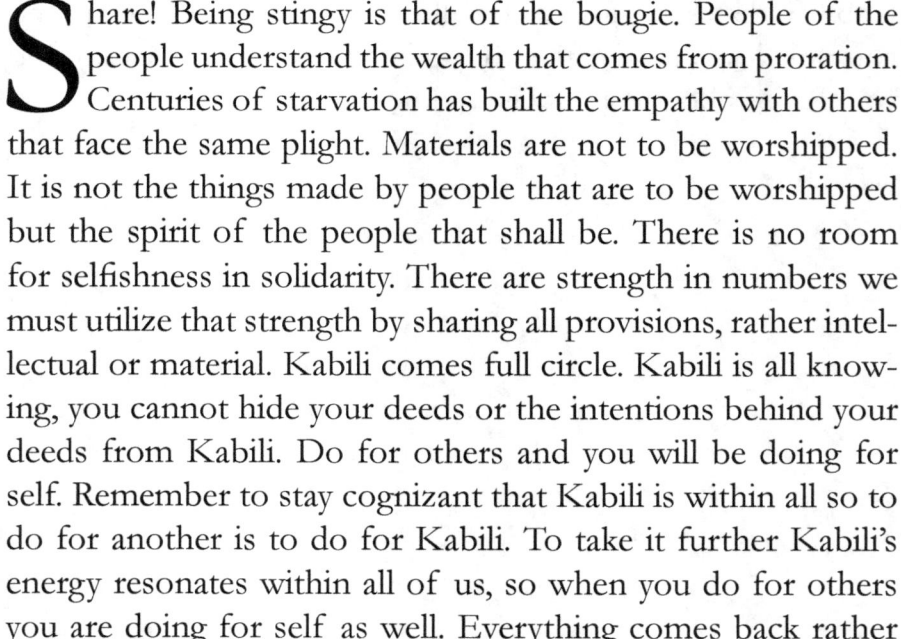

Share! Being stingy is that of the bougie. People of the people understand the wealth that comes from proration. Centuries of starvation has built the empathy with others that face the same plight. Materials are not to be worshipped. It is not the things made by people that are to be worshipped but the spirit of the people that shall be. There is no room for selfishness in solidarity. There are strength in numbers we must utilize that strength by sharing all provisions, rather intellectual or material. Kabili comes full circle. Kabili is all knowing, you cannot hide your deeds or the intentions behind your deeds from Kabili. Do for others and you will be doing for self. Remember to stay cognizant that Kabili is within all so to do for another is to do for Kabili. To take it further Kabili's energy resonates within all of us, so when you do for others you are doing for self as well. Everything comes back rather literal or not. Relationships are to be valued above all else. People of the culture do not know how to be stingy because we've never had anything to be stingy with. This is by design. Eternal bonds are forged through proration and blood. Not material. Material is not the only thing that shall be shared. Knowledge and wisdom as well. One is only as strong as its weakest asset. So everyone must be formidable and trained to be such if it is not innate. Knowledge in the hand of one, is knowledge in the hand of the oppressor. Knowledge in the hand of all, is power to all. So permeate it. When knowledge and wisdom is not passed on throughout the generations, it stifles evolution. "Natural selection" is a product of that generational intelligence. Evolution or extinction? These are the results of being generous with our diamonds or not. If you do not water a seed placed in soil, it will not blossom, eventually it will go extinct but if you be patient with that seed and you water and nourish it even when going through tribulations, the seed shall evolve into a flower and become beautiful. Teach what you know to the next generation. Give them what took you 20 or 30 years to learn in a couple of hours so they will be ahead of their environment and instead of maintaining the culture they will transcend it. What can be a better legacy than to contribute to a legacy of another? One should always seek wealth of intelligence and material but not with selfish motives. The motives shall be communal. We are all brothers and sisters, one eat, we all eat no matter how infinitesimal the provision is. One learn, we all learn there should be no chink in our armor because there will always come a time of war and in a time of war it is imperative to know that the person standing to your left or right will do anything for you. The bond of a diamond is to the death. In every great movement there are dissenters who commonly use the tactic of divide and conquer, do not give credence to these methods in even the most subtle ways. Selfishness being one of them. Selfishness has the power to bring down an empire. Once other start to feel alienated or different, they become alien and different. Accustomed to different customs and morals. They will go against what they know is right to right the wrongs of the ones who made them feel alienated in the first place. By any means necessary. We shall not succumb to this crab in the barrel type thinking. Avoid this by passing the cup, by passing the plate and ultimately by passing the book.

## Chapter 4: Oppression

Who can know state persecution better than us, the culture? The culture tends to always be at the bottom of the caste system. That is why our revolutional spirit is bright. We must never submit ourselves to this persecution willingly. Kabili is firm in the spirit of rebellion for a righteous cause. We must never defile our bodies with governmental experiments or vaccines, to put our temple in jeopardy of degradation by chemicals is unacceptable. Never forget our history of medical persecution by the hands of those that are supposed to heal. Be wary. We do not advocate active violence of the supposed authority; unless you have been transgressed upon. Every human being has the right to defend ones temple and liberty of such. We as the descendants of Kabili are used to being oppressed on by those with the authority but who is to say that is not to be challenged? Never sit by in the face of injustice rather it's been directed at you or not. Never let your integrity or morality be shaken by the many. That in itself is oppression. You must rebel in the face of injustice to save your conscience form mental anguish. If you wake up in the morning and regret yesterday, you know you have done something wrong. So with that being said, live life with no regrets.

Be active in being proactive against evil and injustice. You can expect not to be accepted by mainstream society for our beliefs but when have we ever as participants in our culture been accepted? So don't fret over acceptance. You have it here. You have the support of the diamonds. The diamonds area the masses rather they have been uncovered or not. Stand in solidarity with those that come from the environment and circumstances that you do. These are the only ones that can truly empathize; hence, the only ones that can truly be a part of the culture. Never pay attention to the social caste system when you know who you and your people are and where they stand. Kabili has given resolve to us. That is not to be confused with being content with poverty or the struggle that it brings. Struggle against these conditions by any means. As a human being you have a right to liberty and luxury that is offered to others. You are not destined to be impoverished for luxury. In the next life, as long as you stay motivated and dedicated. With these qualities you will succeed against all forces that seek to stifle your success. There is many in power that profit off the misery of our culture, as well as exploit it. Do not give them the satisfaction. Look to uplift yourself and the culture by your contributions. Always stay cognizant that you are not the only one engaged in this struggle. You have sister and brothers being exploited everywhere. Don't focus on the exploitation of the culture but the solidarity that the exploitation inevitably brings. If we remain united against these forces with hidden agendas, we may change the tide, which is the ultimate goal. To be content is to be stagnant. Growth and development has and shall always be the goal. We have been given a place in society from the time of your birth and our oppressors are working diligently to keep us in that place. The Kabili within you shall awaken with a fiery of rebellion when hearing this. Yet anger is nothing but passion if not used constructively. You must harness this passion and formulate a plan of success.

## Chapter 5: War

War is the price of peace. From the time that Kabili made life possible there has been war. War to live. War to thrive. There will always be a group of people that feel they can impose their will on the masses. With the feeling of indignation the masses will rebel against this. Under these pretenses there is nothing wrong with war as long as it does not become excessive to the point of oppression. We must handle war even handedly but be stern with our enemies. Life is a serious thing and not something to be taken lightly. Therefore be sure before you engage in war that the transgression is worth a life(s). That every means of mediation has been exhausted before engaging in deadly combat. Kabili children are not barbarians, so do not behave like them with a primal instinct steered towards violence. Kabili children have been blessed with wisdom, be perspicacious then in all dealings especially those concerning the death of a fellow human.

Be cognizant that Kabili energy flows through all, connecting you to everyone here on earth, so before taking a brothers/sisters life and piece of Kabili energy, be sure. There is nothing wrong with mediation, only barbarians will think you craven for using your words rather than your sword. As long as you know the reason for peace was not founded out of cowardice, have solace that you spared another knowing what you are capable of. Kabili has given you the power that only he can possess/distribute to create and destroy. Do not abuse it. Kabili will now and will make you pay dearly through karmic energy. Once you are sure that war cannot be mediated and it is inevitable, be meticulous. Be precise. There is no time to waste and war is not for play. Retreat from the domestication that has groomed you and let your instincts that are primordial consume you. The time for thinking is before war, once in war thought should be absent, the body shall become savage. The feeling in your stomach before engaging in combat is butterflies only for the cowards but for the warriors they are fireflies waiting to be released before the roar of the ferocious. War is not to be carried out impulsively, a plan of execution should be made prior to any engagement no matter how small or big. Be secure in your victory before engaging, if you falter in confidence or judgement the war has already been lost. Rely on the strength that Kabili has blessed the righteous with that you will not fall in battle. If you cause is just, and you have exhausted all forms of mediation, and your plan is bulletproof, you shall prevail. Let your heart match your desires. Be valiant. There is nothing wrong about speaking vociferously before engaging in combat. Everyone copes and deals with violence differently. To hear reassurance out loud does not make you a coward as long as you perform when the lights come on. To be silent before violence does not make you fearful, some people enjoy the tranquility of their own mind before combat. In the ancient times of sword and shield battle cries and clamor preluded every battle. To each their own. There is not a book of conduct that is to be followed before war. After the recognition of how fragile life is, is revealed do not become drunk on blood. Do not exploit it weakness with your experience. Continue to be humble in your dealings with people. Don't fall into that pugnacious attitude that many experienced warriors do. You will find yourself running into more problems if you pick up this habit. Be positive, stay positive.

## Chapter 6: Resilience

Stand strong. Never give up. Never surrender. These are the words of Kabilis children. You must be consistent at being resilient. The law of balance will keep negative forces coming at you consistently. You must not bend under the pressure of negativity. You must not dwell on the negative at all. It comes and you should briefly grieve its coming and recover with success. For every negative that happens you shall know by Kabilis law that you are in store for positive. With that knowledge you should be working towards that positive immediately and not worrying about how to cope. Coping means you are still carrying that negative energy with you. This must and shall be released to keep your overall energy positive. Know that we are creatures of habit. If you pick up the habit of not putting your energy into the negative that befits you, you will remain consistent with your positivity. You will have achieved resilience. These are the faculties Kabili has given you. It's up to you to hone them and utilize them. Nothing should keep you down for long. A new day means a new opportunity. It's up to you to go explore them. Kabilis blessings are abundant, go seek them out. We come from the soil never fear getting a little dirty in the pursuit of your happiness. There is no good or bad actions because it's not about what you do but why you do what you do that matters.

## Chapter 7: Vanity

---

Vanity is a weakness. To give credence that one's looks is the value of who they are can be misleading and detrimental to the way one goes about life. Physical appearance is a lot like a jacket because it is a cover. Without doubt that jacket has value but what's important is who is wearing the jacket. The who is what matters, not the what. The flesh is the weak while the character remains strong. Little thought should be given to the weakness of the flesh, instead what should be found intriguing is the strength of one's character. Get to know someone before you judge them on looks alone. Contrary to opinion, Jesus Christ was not a handsome man according to many ancient Roman texts but he inspired a movement that has lasted more than two thousand years. Because it wasn't what he looked like that mattered instead it was what he believed and taught that captured the attention of the masses. Remember that Kabili's children are the church of Diamonds. Before you get to the beauty of a diamond, you must dig and trek through mud and dirt. If we took the gravel at face value we would never have discovered the beauty of a diamond. This is not by chance or coincidence. Kabili has made this so. The metaphorical meanings that Kabili has bestowed upon us always can be found to have an impact upon the literal in some way. Be patient in getting to know ones nature. Don't fall into the ignorance of man by being manipulated by a pretty face or mesmerizing eyes. Judge on by the principles of morality. Observe and listen, only then will you know the true beauty of someone. You may rob yourself of blessings if you judge a book by its cover. Instead take your time to read the synopsis.

## Chapter 8: Loyalty

Loyalty is not something to be taken lightly. One should not give it easily or accept it without lengthy consideration. Loyalty ties you to someone and has the power to intertwine destinies. Be wary of who you give your loyalty if not for any other reason than that. Most people will not be deserving of your loyalty. Not because most people are bad but because most people are for self. Loyalty has the power to bridge gaps while destroying other bridges in the meantime. Loyalty once given should not be something that's conditional because once given you have already took on the responsibility of this person and everything that comes along with that person. From the good to the bad. The good of course will be beneficial but unlike the bad that comes with that person it will be temporary. If the loyalty is founded upon conditions, you will inherit this person's problems and drama as well and some will be life lasting. The universe does not know conditions, the universe knows to give you what you have created. Once you have carefully decided who will be the recipients of your loyalty do not be fickle in nature. Ensure that your loyalty is not only worthy but means something. Be there for that person in every way whenever they are in time of need of anything. The only time it is acceptable to not provide for the recipient of your loyalty in their time of need, is when your aid will be used to go against your moral principles. At that time, loyalty mandates that you have a meeting of the mind with this person. A compromise shall be made without compromising your principles for the sake of your loyalty. Once again loyalty shall not be conditional. At no time rather this person goes against your moral principles or not are you to report this person to the powers to be. One shall not advocate the involvement of the government in communal problems, regardless of the deed. Loyalty to a diamond shall be given under the sanctity of Kabili. Kabili has made you brother and sister, to forsake your obligations of kinship shall be a sin. Be to others, what you want people to be to you. It starts with you and what you project. With the thoughts of loyalty being the same for all diamonds, one has no worry of what will be received, because you know what you are giving to a likeminded individual. To gossip behind ones back or to tell ones business to others is not loyalty. Even if all are mutual friends. If told in confidence respect yourself and the confidence that one has in you. If one is not in position to be there for their loved ones make sure that your loyalty extends to them as well and do for them what your friend would be doing but can't due to the position one is in. Come together in solidarity in these times and make sure no one is forgotten. Make sure that if this person does not have it but you do, that you contribute to their prosperity rather than contributing to their stagnation or regression. Do not play favorites or choose sides with those that you have given your loyalty to. Stay true. This is the expectations and meaning of loyalty.

## Chapter 9: The Devil

The Devil is the negative energy that permeates throughout you and the universe. Therefore you are a product of the devil and have a piece of the devil within you. Just as you have a piece of Kabili within you. There is no positive without negative and vice versa. These are dual realities. There is nothing wrong with the devil because it is just as natural as Kabili itself. You are the combination of both, forming the ultimate deity, you have the power to create which is the power Kabili has bestowed upon you. You have the power to destroy which is the power that the devil has bestowed upon you. By the devil being the rod of everything negative it is integral to the balance of life that forms the law of balance. Reverse such a great power but remain consistent in your belief of Kabili the creator as Kabili has remained consistent in creation. Kabili created the devil with the intentions of forming the ultimate balance. The stigma surrounding the devil is that it is an evil and malicious entity. That could not be the farthest thing from the truth. Mankind uses the negative energy that the devil provides to be evil and malicious against one another. It is not the energy itself that is evil. How can a necessity be evil? The devil is a necessity of universal balance. Remaining positive is to reside in the web of Kabili, safe from negativity that passes through one's mind. Your judgement of the devil is irrelevant, after the judgement subsides, it is still itself, free of emotion, or will.

## Chapter 10: Constructive Criticism

Be receptive of constructive criticism. Do not become so arrogant as to think that you are above reproach. All of Kabili's children are a perfect construction of Kabili's ultimate plan for the universe. That does not mean one has immediately honed the skills that they have been blessed with. We are direct products of our earlier domestication. Maybe that motivation is auspicious to the qualities one has been blessed with. Maybe it is not. No matter what, although perfectly constructed for the universe, no one will be perfect in the standards of society. There is no law of a diamond that says one must exist to appease society but it is the standard of a diamond to be humble and gracious in every dealing. To be righteous and just, seeing that you are a representative of something bigger than yourself. That reflection has to be identical of our beliefs and principles. If you are consistently being admonished by multiple people for the same thing, maybe just maybe, these people are not all just nitpicking things in your personality. Maybe you or your actions are the problem and after proper deliberation, if this comes back to have a ring of truth to it, honor yourself by honing your qualities. This comes back to growth and development. Never be content with being stagnant. If you are not on a consistent path of growth, indeed you are remaining stagnant. If you think that there is no room for growth in your character, inevitably your character will become stunted by stagnation. So look for growth before someone points it out to you! Be proactive and being a better you. If necessary, ask friends what do they find difficult in your personality and be genuine in your curiosity. After deep introspection if you believe that you can be a better human, better person, better diamond, by mending your short-coming, do so without hesitation. Kabili will put people in your path with the intentions of you two learning and growing from each other. When you encounter someone who challenges you mentally, intellectually and emotionally without toxicity revel in that. Take it for what it is, the critical thinking of building character. Don't waste your time by being wasteful of your blessings. Dig your heels in and allow yourself to learn and grow form this challenge. Ask questions, change patterns, challenge mindsets, seek new career opportunities, etc. The only cap on your growth is the gap given by you.

## Chapter 11: Tribe and Contribution

There is no one man above the community unless appointed by the community. This chieftain has responsibilities to keep his people safe, fed and sheltered. The chieftain must always put his community's wellbeing before his or anyone else's. There is no chief without Indians though. The community must rally behind the chief. Trusting in the vision that this person appointed rather you know the desired outcome or not. When talking about the longevity of a structure, the carrying out of orders is essential. The structure only stands as long as it is respected. Once disrespected, it is noticed by everyone and slowly but surely those boundaries start to break down. Now an every man for himself type of motto is adopted and there is no communal. How can there be evolution without mutual aid? Mutual aid is a must in humanity, especially when humanity is building a community. Therefore structure is necessity of any concerted effort. The people must be organized with leadership and leadership must be progressive. Not stagnant. As an individual must be willing to give to the collective before one ever thinks about receiving from the collective. If you are contemplating the fruits of labor without actually doing any labor, then you have the chronological order of the maxim wrong. Only consider what you can contribute when contemplating a collective or community. Thinking about what can be gained shows a motive of selfishness. There is no room for selfishness in a community. This person has a natural disposition to order that is not favorable to an organized collective. Expel this person immediately before they are given the chance to sow discord amongst the community. All it takes is one disgruntled person to start a movement. Be vigilant of the poison and bringers of such. Be wary of the slackers that are only around to hitch a ride on the bandwagon. Do not be fooled by the false words of commitments. Everyone sounds the same before their sincerity is put to the test. The people who are committed to the cause will demonstrate so through sacrifice and bloodshed. By the will of Kabili has mankind been in tribes since the beginning to thrive and succeed in the natural selection process. We are tribesman. Naturally to do for the community is a primordial instinct that we will never be able to rid ourselves of. Do not disconnect from your humanity for selfishness. Contribute! What to do for others. Do not occupy a community without contributing to it. This is the action of a leech. Be noble and have noble intentions for your collective. Seek more by wanting more. Achieve more by contributing more. Crowd energy is a real thing, set in the universe by Kabili. Indolence will and can be felt by the community. Do not unintentionally hinder your communities' progress by being complacent. As a chieftain one must be must more dedicated to these principles than anybody else in the collective. The people will be looking to you for guidance not just on matters of state but on matters of conduct as well. What is okay and what is not. How must my approach be in all things of community? With a thousand eyes upon you, you must be critical of self before every action. Must be prudent enough to discern when action should be taken or inaction should be taken. The next generation of chieftains are watching. Kabili has made empiricism so. Do not disregard this blessing by misusing it against the youth. Know what is being taught and make sure progress of the community is at the forefront. First a chieftain must be wise. Then and only then is the chieftain a warrior. One must have the patience to gauge a situation carefully before acting. One must be perspicacious enough to decipher a truth from a likely falsehood. The order of the people should come directly through the chieftain proxy his commanders. The community of Kabili's followers must be organized as a state. A qualified person must be able to find the director and trajectory of the church, as well as being able to stand up to the persecution of the state that is sure to follow. Wisdom and strength are traits that are required to lead. Lead from the front. Those chieftains are the respected. Never ask your people to do what you are not willing to do. Once it is known that you have done this, they will lose respect for you. If they do not respect you they will not follow you. The commitment to community is our key to prosperity.

# Chapter 12: No judgement/hate

One must be committed to loving all with the only exception being the enemies of Kabili's culture and lifestyle. This does not give permission to hate others. No one should be hated unless they have broken commandments 2, 3, 4, 6, or 7. Acceptance of all, even to those that do not follow our lifestyle, should be extended to all. To hate one without merit is ignorance. TO hate one because they are in opposition to our beliefs is close minded. Everyone is entitled to their own belief system without pressure from anyone. Be prudent, but be inclusive. Love is the cure for the disease of hate. Hate is the product of negativity, allowed to flow unchecked it can and will consume you. People look to hate one another for lack of understanding but the wise have understanding for all things. All that's left to be considered is what will be tolerated. What should not make the tolerable list is hate. Even when one is at odds with the next, the thought of hate should not be the result. To have to succumb to such passion to dislike one demonstrates the weakness in one's character. Kabili's children are the strong and chosen.

## Chapter 13: Betrayal

---

Betrayal is a trait of the weak. Never succumb to innate desires. If you can't stand strong in the face of adversity what is the difference between you and a coward? It will not always be easy to stand on principle. Sometimes it will be the hardest road to take. The road might be full of desert and cactus for as far as you can see and the compromise road is full of flowers and wellsprings but this is where strength of character plays a role. You must be strong and Kabili will bless you for your resilience and perseverance because his vision goes much further than yours. The weak may be rewarded with material possession but Kabili will curse their spirit by creating mental turmoil. Weakness is a disease. Curable? Yes, but only by way of sacrifice and dedication. Nothing in the universe comes free due to the law of balance. It's always something attached to it rather it be in the now or the far future. Stay true to your beliefs and your loved ones. Loyalty is rewarded. Betrayal is despised by all including the objective of Kabili. The easiness in things is a mirage. Including betrayal. It comes with spiritual tumult and moral depravation. Once one card folds the whole pyramid is subject to collapse. Keep the house intact by keeping your morals intact.

# BOOK OF DIAMONDS

# CHURCH OF DIAMONDS

# Prophets of Principles

# CHURCH OF DIAMONDS

# 1: Jack Johnson — Prophet of Principle

John "Jack" Arthur Johnson, was a black man born March 31st 1878 (15 years after slavery had formally ended) in Galveston, Texas to former slaves Henry and Tina Johnson. His father "Henry" was a war veteran and his mother "Tina" was a dish washer, respectfully. Growing up in Galveston, Texas, Johnson only attended five years of school. Growing up in rural Galveston, Texas at the time he was not affected by segregation. He made friends with white boys, even sleeping over at some of their houses. His youthful experiences molded his mindset of equality where he was quoted as saying "No one ever taught me that white men were superior to me." His first few jobs were exercising horses and a carriage painter with his last job being a janitor at a boxing gym. After that he began what was known as "Cellar Fighting" where one was to fight in a basement type setting in front of small crowds for a purse, as prize fighting was still illegal in Texas at the time he was jailed a couple of times for this. He made his first professional boxing debut November 1st, 1898, where he knocked out Charley Brooks in the second round of a 15 round match. On February 25th, 1901 Johnson fought popular heavyweight Joe Choynski and was knocked out in the third round. As prizefighting was still illegal at the time in Texas, they were both jailed and held on $5,000 bail. The sheriff permitted both boxers to go home at night if they would agree to spar in a jail cell in front of spectators. Which they did. Johnson was in jail for 23 days before grand jury refused to indict. Johnson later stated that he learned his boxing skills during that jail time. Johnson became the world colored heavy weight champion on February 3rd, 1903 after defeating Denver Ed Martin by decision in a 20 round match. Johnson held the title until it was vacated in 1908 when he beat Tommy Burns for world heavy weight title by "TKO" in Sydney Australia. Johnson had to pester him for two years following him around the world and taunting him before Tommy Burns agreed to fight the black man for the heavyweight championship. For two years, former undefeated champion James J. Jefferies agreed to come out of retirement to fight Jack Johnson to defend the white race and show its superiority. On July 4th, 1910, in the 15th round after Jefferies had been knocked down twice for the first time in his career, Jefferies corner threw in the towel. Afterwards Jefferies was humbled by the loss stating "I could never have whipped Johnson at my best. No, I couldn't have touched him in a 1,000 years." On April 5th, 1915, Johnson lost his title to Jess Willard in Havana, Cuba. Johnson fought professionally until 1937, at the time he was 60 years old. Johnson was persecuted by the racist media as well as the government for his marriages and relationships with white women. Which led him to eventually be charged, tried and convicted of the "Mann Act" forbidding one to transport a woman across state lines for an immoral purpose. He was sentenced to a year in Leavenworth before going on the run for seven years abroad, until 1920 when he returned and served his time. He died in a car crash on June 10th, 1946 at the age of 68 in Franklin, NC. Jack Johnson was a man of principle and in an era of black oppression and segregation didn't allow anyone to dictate his movements and actions. He honed the rebellious spirit of Kabili and walked with his head held high in the face of hate even serving jail time to demonstrate he was a free man free to choose a partner of his liking. He carried himself with swagger of the culture, even having a mouth full of golds in the first decade of the 20th century. Something that was not yet fashionable in the black culture. Honor him and the principle he stood one: courage.

## 2: Raymond Washington — Prophet of Principle

Raymond Lee Washington was a black man born on August 14th, 1953 in Los Angeles, California to Violet Samuel and Reginald Washington. He grew up on the eastside of South Central on 76th street and Central Avenue. Growing up Raymond had a difficult childhood, engaging in local mischief and neighborhood fistfights. His youthful activities kept him in trouble with the law resulting in several expulsions throughout his high school years. Eventually Raymond became involved in street gangs leading him to start his own gang that he named Crip. To set his gang apart from others at the time, he created a variety of things that were unique to only them. For example: he created a dance called the Crip walk, designated the left side as the Crip side where all things were to be worn such as: earrings, bandannas (The blue bandanna had been selected as the battle flag of the Crips), gloves, etc. TO focus on the expansion and denomination of the Los

Angeles streets he struck a deal agreeing to a confederacy with Stanley "Tookie" Williams that represented the Westside. Together they solidified the Crips as a cornerstone of gang culture in Los Angeles by violently dealing with their enemies. Five years after starting Crip, Raymond was sent to prison for robbery which he received a five year term for in 1974. During his incarceration it is widely accepted that he had a relatively tumultuous stay. The pro-black organizations ran the prisons and had been established there for many years and were not fans of what they viewed as self-genocide spearheaded by Raymond Washington. So just existing in these institutions as the founder of Crip put a target on his back. When released from prison he noticed Crip was not the same organization that he had started. It now had many splinter factions that broke down the overall authority of the gang. Realizing that there was no future on this path he began to vocalize that he wanted to reunite all the Crips under one umbrella and call a truce with their rivals: Bloods. Before his wish was able to come to fruition he was gunned down at 10:00pm on August 9th, 1979 on the eastside of South Central. Since then Raymond's legacy lives on through all the Crips that came after him. Raymond was a young black man that grew up in the streets of South Central where fighting was a way of life. If you were not fighting against local bullies you were fighting against law enforcement. He took what he knew and aspired to be bigger than his section. Regardless if one agrees with his route to infamy you must recognize the principle of: Ambition! Wanting more than your environment or situation. One thing that cannot be argued is that he took his skills of leadership and violent prowess and became international. Honor him and the principle he stood on: Ambition.

## 3: Muhammad Ali — Prophet of Principle

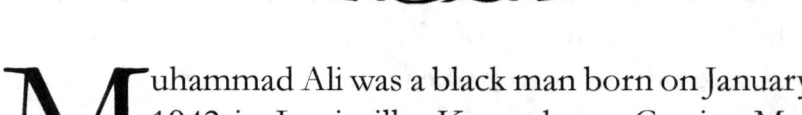

Muhammad Ali was a black man born on January 17th, 1942 in Louisville, Kentucky to Cassius Marcellus Clay Sr. and Odessa Grady Clay. Ali's childhood was relatively quiet. He grew up in a household that had both parents and one brother. He grew up dyslexic which led to frustrations in school work. At the age of twelve Ali was encountered by a cop after having his bike stolen. He told the officer that if he saw the thief he would "whoop" him in which the officer responded "You better learn how to box first." After seeing amateur fights on TV he decided to take him up on his offer and began training. Ali made his amateur boxing debut in 1954 in which he won by split decision. He went on to win six Kentucky "Golden Gloved" titles, two national "Golden Gloves" titles, one amateur athletic union title and the light heavy weight gold medal in the 1960 Summer Olympics. After winning in the Olympics he turned professional where he won the heavy weight championship multiple times with his first time coming on February 25th, 1964 against Sonny Liston. At the age of 22, Ali converted to Islam. Specifically the nation of Islam faction. After doing so he changed his name from Cassius Clay Jr. to Muhammad Ali. In the time before voting rights for African Americans this caused a huge controversy especially being a part of the "NOI" who were dubbed the "Black Muslims" at the time by the media reporters and boxers alike refused to call him his newly changed name. Which only incensed him all the more who viewed his previous name as his slave name. In 1966 Ali refused to be drafted in the military to go fight in the Vietnam War citing religious beliefs and ethical opposition to the war. He was against going overseas to kill people that had never caused him any harm and was famously quoted as saying "they ain't never called me no nigger." He became the center piece of America's hate and was notoriously called unpatriotic by many and a coward by others for refusing to be drafted. He was also stripped of his heavy weight title. He stayed out of prison by appealing his conviction which was eventually overturned by the Supreme Court. Although he won his case he sacrificed almost 4 years out of his boxing career to stand on his principle. He eventually won the title again but widely accepted that he was never the same fighter. In 1981 Ali retired from boxing and focused on philanthropy, religion, and activism. He died June 3rd, 2016 from complications with Parkinson's syndrome. Ali endured hate form the masses for the majority of his life for standing up for what he believed in. Rather that was race, religion, or war he never wavered. He showed the whole world what principle was and how to stand on it. For that honor him and the principle he stood on: Principle.

## 4: David Barksdale — Prophet of Principle

King David was a black man born on May 24th, 1947 in Sallis, Mississippi to Virginia and Charlie Barksdale. King David had twelve other siblings and was raised in Mississippi until moving to Chicago, Illinois in 1957. By 1972 King David was recognized as the undisputed leader of the "Black Disciples Nation." In 1968 King David was shot seven times by a rival gang member while sitting in his car. In 1970 King David was shot again while exiting a bar. King David was a constant target while running his empire leading him to propose and create a merger with then leader of the "gangster disciple's nation" to form the "Black Gangster Disciples Nation". King David was and still is revered in his city for being a man that stood on principle even if it meant forfeiting his life. On September 2nd, 1974 King David died from Kidney failure as a result of lead poisoning that occurred from being shot.

## 5: Angela Davis — Prophet of Principle

Angela Davis was a black woman born on January 26th, 1944 in Birmingham, Alabama. She grew up in what was known as "Dynamite Hill" by many which got its name from the bombing of black people houses in order to intimidate and eradicate. Growing up in the late 40's and 50's she experienced racism every day. From going to the store or school and also seeing friends she went to school with die in racially motivated bombings. Her parents were communist and organizers for the communist party which allowed her to garner knowledge from a very young age about societal and economic issues. In her junior years of high school she was accepted by a Quaker program that placed black students from the south in integrated school in the north. While there she joined a youth communist group called "Advance". After high school she was accepted into Brandeis University in Massachusetts where she was only one of three black people in her class. During her second year in college she went to college in France to study French. After graduating from Brandeis she went to the University of Frankfurt for graduate work in philosophy. While in Germany she participated in radical movements, primarily with the "Socialist German Student Union" against the West Germans who were still dealing with widespread fascism. After two years in Germany she returned to the states where she got involved with numerous political groups: Che Lumumba Club, Black Panther Party, and the SNCC. While engaging in political activity in California she began to work as a professor at the University of California, Los Angeles (UCLA). While working there the University enacted a policy against hiring communists at the behest of Ronald Reagan himself. With this policy in place they fired Angela Davis in which she appealed and the courts ruled she cannot be fired solely off of her political affiliation with the communist party. A year later the University found excuse to fire her which they called "inflammatory language" she had used in four different speeches. While engaged in political activity in support of the Soledad brothers Jonathon Jackson (the seventeen year old brother of Soledad brother George Jackson) took control of a Marin County courthouse in an attempt to liberate two black defendants that were on trial. They took five hostages including the judge and prosecutor. Outside the courthouse a shootout ensued in the getaway vehicle that ended with the judge and all three black men being murdered. An investigation revealed Angela Davis had purchased several of the firearms used just two days before the attempted liberation. An arrest warrant was issued for her with a sleuth of charges including but not limited to capital murder. After two months on the run she was caught in New York City and extradited back to California to stand trial. With the help of millions of people and many countries that started a "free Angela" movement she was acquitted on all charges two years later. Her incarceration led to her being one of the most famous people in the world at the time. After her release she continued to engage in political activity perhaps even more vigorously now. She went on a worldwide speaking tour against political repression and state sanctioned oppression. In the USSR she received an honorary doctorate from Moscow State University she was also awarded the Lenin Peace Prize from the Soviet Union. Angela Davis also continued to teach around the country at various schools. Sometimes being discriminated against by administration by limiting or minimizing her role in campus activities. Still in 2022 Angela Davis is active in political activity. She has not rested and has continued to fight against the injustices of racism, sexism, imperialism and modern day slavery. For that we must honor her and the principle she stands on: perseverance!

## 6: Malcom X – Prophet of Principle

Malcom X was a black man born on May 19th, 1925 to Louise Helen Little and Earl Little in Omaha, Nebraska. Growing up Malcom X was inculcated in black political activism because his parents were a part of Marcus Garvey's "Universal Negro Improvement Association". Race was polarized to Malcom in his youth by losing four of his uncles and his father to what he believed to be racial violence. When he was thirteen years old his mother had a nervous breakdown and because his father had died seven years earlier he and his siblings were sent to foster homes in the state of Michigan. From 14 to 18 Malcom held a variety of jobs while staying with his sister in Boston. He moved to Harlem, New York in 1943 and got a job at the New Haven Railroad. While working there he engaged in a variety of criminal activities. When he was summoned by the local draft board during World War II he feigned mental illness and was declared "mentally disqualified for military service." In 1946 Malcom was arrested for larceny and breaking and entering for burglarizing homes in the Boston area. He was given 8-10 years. While in prison Malcom X was introduced to the nation of Islam by a plethora of people including but not limited to the leader of the nation at the time, Elijah Muhammad. He began a spiritual transformation while in prison. He stopped smoking cigarettes and eating pork. He began to read voraciously, including the entire dictionary. He dedicated his life to the nation of Islam and left criminality in his past. Upon his release he began ministering for the nation of Islam and did so well that he expanded their numbers and was ultimately promoted to the leading minister of the nation. During his dozen years with the nation of Islam he preached the doctrine that white people were devils. After completing his Hajj to Mecca he was enlightened after seeing different races embrace him as a brother of Islam. Due to this change in belief and a number of other things he renounced the nation of Islam and made his own organization called "Muslim Mosque, Inc." where he continued to preach black excellence and progress. During this time the FBI ramped up their more than ten year surveillance of him and began to instigate conflict between him and the nation. While preaching in the Audubon Ballroom in Harlem, New York on February 21, 1965 he was assassinated by three gunmen, two of which have been acquitted. It was and still is controversy on the U.S. Government being involved in his slaying. In his almost forty years of life Malcom X exhibited racial pride at all times. He fought for the liberation of his people in his words "By any means necessary". Honor him and the principle he stood on: pride.

# 7: Che Guevara – Prophet of Principle

Ernesto "Che" Guevara was an Argentinian-Cuban man born May 14th, 1928 to Ernesto Guevara Lynch and Celia de la Sema y Llosa in Rosario, Santa Fe province, Argentina. Che grew up in a leftist household. His father was a supporter of the veterans who fought in the Spanish Civil War on the Republican side. Despite having asthma he was very involved with sports throughout his life from swimming, football, golf, and bicycling. He was also an avid and eclectic reader growing up. His home growing up had more than 3,000 books in it. He became familiar with his political ideology at this time form reading Karl Marx. As a young man he became a medical student that traveled throughout South America. While abroad he was radicalized by the poverty, hunger, and disease that he saw. His humanitarian exploits eventually led him to Mexico City where he met the pioneers of the Cuban Revolution Raul and Fidel Castro. There he joined their revolution and traveled to Cuba with them on their yacht with the intention of overthrowing the then Cuban dictator Fulgencio Batista. His wit and courage led him to prominence among the revolutionaries earning him a promotion to second in command in the Cuban Revolutionary Armed forces. After the two yearlong successful Cuban Revolution he played numerous roles in the New Communist Government, including but not limited to the revolutionary tribunals for war criminals, minister of industries, spearheading a successful literacy campaign, national bank president, and a worldwide diplomat on behalf of Cuba. His studies and experiences led him to the belief that the only way to reverse the third worlds underdevelopment and dependency was with worldwide revolution. With this belief in 1965 he left Cuba to engage in and encourage continental revolution across both Africa and South America. He fought unsuccessfully to liberate the Congo. Afterwards he went and fought in Bolivia's revolution where he was eventually captured by Bolivian forces. After fighting in numerous battles including the attack on El Uvero, Operation Verano, Battle of Las Mercedes, Battle of Santa Clara, Bay of Pigs Invasion, Cuban Missile Crisis, Congo Crisis, and the Bolivian Campaign, he was executed by firing squad by the Bolivian Forces on October 9th, 1967. He lived for the people and gave his life for the people. He traveled the world seeking to liberate others form their oppressors. He was a brilliant mind that was not afraid to take to violence in defense of freedom. For this honor him and the principle he stood on: altruism.

## 8: Griselda Blanco Restrepo — Prophet of Principle

Griselda Blanco Restrepo was a Colombian woman born on February 15th, 1943 to Ana Lucia Restrepo and Fernando Blanco in Cartagena, Bolivar, Colombia. At the age of three her and her mother moved to Medellin where Griselda grew up in extreme poverty. She began her criminal career early in the hopes of attaining money. At the age of eleven she carried out her first kidnapping for ransom. Eventually shooting the victim to encourage the family to pay. In the mid 1970's Griselda Blanco and her second husband immigrated to Queens, New York by using fake passports. They established a lucrative cocaine business by importing the drug from Colombia using female couriers by sending them through airports with the drug being stashed in their bra and panties. In 1975, her and 30 of her subordinates were indicted on federal drug charges but before she could be arrested she fled to Colombia where she continued to run her drug empire.

She returned to the states in the late 70's, settling in Miami. Before she returned though she was alleged to have killed her husband in a Bogota nightclub parking lot for stealing millions from her. At the conclusion of the shootout she was left shot in the abdomen while her husband and six of his bodyguards lay dead. She was alleged to have killed 3 out of her 4 husbands. Either directly by her hands or the carrying out of her orders. While in Miami she expanded her network throughout the country until her business brought in more than eighty million a month. She is largely attributed with being responsible for the "Cocaine Cowboy Wars" that took place throughout the eighties in Miami. Public executions was the way she handled wars, bringing attention to herself and her empire. After repeated attempts on her life in Miami she moved to California where she continue to run her empire. On February 18th, 1985 Griselda was arrested for drug trafficking at her home and held without bail. While awaiting trial she met a young man from Oakland that was a drug dealer. He reached out to her via letter, afterwards they began a sexual relationship with her bribing the guards for alone time for the two of them. This relationship led to her putting him and her son in charge of her drug empire. While fighting her case they were indicted on more drug charges in Miami with these charges ultimately being dropped due to a sex scandal between a star witness and a female secretary. In the District Attorneys' Office Griselda was sentenced to almost 2 decades in prison in 2004. She was deported back to Medellin, Colombia upon release. She kept a low profile while free knowing that her exploits with Pablo Escobar and the Medellin Cartel had made her many enemies. On September 3rd, 2012, she was shot twice (once in the head) while shopping, by a gunman on the back of a motorcycle.

Griselda Blanco died on the scene at the age of 69. Griselda showed her hustle by becoming the first female criminal billionaire. She chased her bag by any means necessary and lived a life of luxury until her incarceration. She carved out her own place in history by being a go-getter. For this honor her and the principle she stood on: hustle.

## 9: Assata Shakur — Prophet of Principle

Assata Olugbala Shakur was a black woman born on July 16th, 1947 to Doris. E. Johnson in Queens, New York. At the age of three Assata moved with her grandparents to Wilmington, North Carolina. After completing elementary in North Carolina, Assata returned to Queens to live with her mother. She began to have problems at home which led to her running away frequently until she was taken in by her aunt. She began to engage in political activities in the mid 1960's while attending community college. She was arrested for the first time with a hundred other students for chaining the entrance door shut to a building in the college to protest the lack of black faculty and black studies. After graduating from community college she moved to Oakland, California where she joined the Black Panther Party. She returned to New York soon after, where she led the BPP chapter in Harlem where she coordinated the free breakfast program for children, free clinics, and community outreach. Assata soon left the party for having differing opinions with the leadership. She then joined the Black Liberation Army which was a clandestine revolutionary group that carried out armed struggle against the U.S. Government. They engaged in bombing government buildings, assassinating police officers, killing drug dealers, and robbing banks. In the beginning of 1971 Assata went on the run after having warrants issued for arrest for bank robberies and multiple assaults on officers. During this time she continued to be dedicated to both the class and black struggle while on the run. She was eventually shot in a hotel room in April of 1971 over some sort of dispute. When she was questioned about it she refused to elaborate. She was arrested and booked into jail until ultimately she was released on bond. In May of 1973, while on the run, her and two other members of the Black Liberation Army (Zayd Malik Shakur and Sundiata Acoli) were pulled over on a New Jersey turnpike. A shootout ensued that left Zayd Shakur and a state trooper dead, while Assata herself was shot multiple times. The lone surviving officer stated that they were fired upon first and were only acting in self-defense. Assata was charged with Murder, attempted murder, armed robbery, bank robbery, and kidnapping. She was acquitted on all cases except for the New Jersey turnpike shooting. In 1977 she was convicted of murder and seven other felonies related to the New Jersey turnpike shooting. While serving a life sentence she escaped from prison in 1979. She resurfaced in 1984, in Cuba where she had been granted political asylum. The U.S. Government worked continuously to get her back in custody to no avail. In 2013 she was put on the FBI's most wanted terrorist list with a two million dollar bounty on her head Assata continues to live free in Cuba and has even gave a few interviews since her escape. Assata is renowned in the black community for going to war for black rights and denying justice. The rapper Tupac Shakur was her godson and always spoke highly of her. Assata never folded under the pressure of the law even when being held in chains. Assata fought for freedom and continues to fight for hers. While being subjected to multiple man hunts she showed she was built for it by never giving in or giving up. For this honor her and the principle she stood on: resilience.

## 10: Fidel Castro — Prophet of Principle

———⊶o⌒⌒o⊷———

Fidel Alejandro Castro Ruz was a Cuban man born on August 13th, 1926 to Angel Castro y Argiz, in Biran, Cuba. Fidel Castro had a relatively quiet childhood. He was the son of a wealthy farmer. He went to school to study law at the University of Havana, where he eventually became a lawyer. In college is where he became radicalized and adopted antiimperialist views. He went on to participate in rebellions throughout Latin America including the Dominican Republic and Colombia, taking on fascist governments. He returned home with the hopes of overthrowing the then Cuban president Fulgencio Batista, launching a failed attack on the Moncada Barracks in 1955. After a year's imprisonment, Fidel traveled to Mexico where he eventually formed the Revolutionary group the "26th of July Movement" with his brother Raul Castro and prophet Ernesto "Che" Guevara. They returned to Cuba to lead the Cuban Revolution by leading the

Guerilla War Movement against Batista's forces. Fidel and his movement overthrew Batista in 1959 and Fidel assumed military and political power as Cuba's Prime Minister. Fidel Castro then converted the country into a one party Socialist State under the communist party. He introduced policies of free education and healthcare. He nationalized Cuba's industry and business. As Capitalists the U.S. Government was opposed to this and unsuccessfully sought to remove him from power by way of assassination, economic blockade, and counter-revolution including the "Bay of Pigs Invasion" of 1961. Fidel Castro countered all of these attempts and aligned Cuba with the Soviet Union and allowed the Soviets to place nuclear weapons in Cuba resulting in the "Cuban Missile Crisis" (a defining incident of the Cold War) in 1962. Fidel Castro led the country until 2008. Fidel Castro maintained himself as a revolutionary throughout his whole life, sending troops all over the world to aid in liberation form oppression. Under constant threat of death he never wavered from his dedication to his people to never see exploitation and imperialism again. Throughout his entire life, no matter the circumstances, he stayed loyal to the cause. For this honor him and the principle he stood on: loyalty.

## 11: JEFF FORT — PROPHET OF PRINCIPLE

Jeff Fort is a black man born February 20th, 1947 to John Lee and Annie Fort in Aberdeen, Mississippi. As a young boy Jeff Fort moved to Chicago. He had a hard time in school because he suffered from dyslexia. At the time teachers did not know how to work with students that had dyslexia, so in place of school he began to run the streets. He became a prominent figure in the community because of his criminal activities. He eventually co-founded the street gang "Black P. Stone". They specialized in robberies and extortion, demanding payment for protection from prostitutes and drug dealers. At the age of 22 he began to receive deferral grant money to employ ex-cons in the urban community. The job programs come under investigation after accusations that the grant money was being diverted into criminal activities. Fort was subpoenaed to testify before a Senate committee. Fort introduced himself to the committee and then walked out. For this he was convicted of contempt of congress. In 1972, Fort was sentenced to five years in prison. After his release from prison he moved to Milwaukee, Wisconsin and joined the "Moorish Science Temple." Fort then renamed his faction of the Black P. Stones to the "El Rukn Tribe of the Moorish Science of Temple". El Rukn meaning "Pillar" in Arabic. He returned to Chicago soon after and purchased "The Oakwood" an old vacant movie theater, that he renamed "the Fort." The gang began to traffic in cocaine and heroin under his direction. In 1983, he was eventually convicted of drug trafficking and given 13 years. Four years later Jeff Fort was convicted of Domestic terrorism and sentenced to 80 years for instructing members of El Rukn to carry out attacks against the U.S. for weapons and 2.5 million dollars for the Libyan Government. In 1988 he was convicted of yet another sentence for ordering the murder of a rival gang member, for this he was given 75 years. Bringing his total sentence to a 168 years. When the federal supermax prison ADX in Florence, Colorado was opened in 2006 he was sent there to serve his time and put under a no human contact order for the rest of his life. Throughout his entire life, Jeff Fort demonstrated persistence in seeking to become bigger than his environment. He never stopped trying to generate wealth and uplift those around. Jeff Fort always went above and beyond in every plan he formulated, no matter how many times he got knocked down. For this honor him and the principle he stands on: persistence.

## 12: Stanley "Tookie" Williams – Prophet of Principle

Tookie was a black man born on December 29th, 1953, in New Orleans, Louisiana. In 1959, he and his mother moved to South Central, California. As Tookie's mom worked several jobs to support them, he became a latchkey kid and engaged in mischief on the streets. While hanging out in the streets older people in the neighborhood would make the youth fight, including Tookie himself, and pay them if they won. Eventually, Tookie earned a formidable reputation in the neighborhood leading to older kids trying to bully him forcing him to carry a switchblade for protection. In high school Tookie was expelled from school and black balled by several others for fighting. At the age of 15 he joined a neighborhood clique on the west side of South Central and eventually earned the clique's respect for beating up a member for disrespecting his mother. He eventually became the leader as his violent reputation spread around the city. At sixteen he was arrested for car theft and sent to Los Padrinos Juvenile hall where he was introduced to Olympic weightlifting by the gym coach there. Throughout his life this affinity with body building stayed. After doing approximately a year and a half he was released at seventeen. When the review board asked him what he planned to do, he replied "Being the leader of the biggest gang in the world." He met Raymond Washington soon after his release and joined the Crips gang with the agreement being he would lead the Westside faction. He began to live a double life, where he worked as an anti-gang youth counselor, studied sociology at Compton College, and engaged in violent crimes against his rivals. In 1976, Tookie was a victim of a drive-by shooting in front of his house. He was shot in both legs and told by the doctors he would never walk again. After a year of physical rehabilitation and intense workout regimen he gained his ability to walk again. Soon after he began using PCP heavily, even having such a bad psychotic break downs that he was committed to a mental institution for a short period of time. He eventually lost his job as a youth counselor for being implicated in a robbery. He was also denied the chance to compete at an amateur bodybuilding contest after it was revealed that he was a gang leader. In 1979, he was charged with four murders for two different armed robberies. He was found guilty of murdering one store clerk and three motel clerks. In 1981, Tookie was then placed on death row in San Quentin State Prison located in San Quentin, California. In the 1990's he denounced the Crip gang and began to write children's books hoping to divert them from gang activity. He spoke to kids around the world on gang prevention, hoping to spare them from the reality he was living. After 26 years of incarceration and 24 years of being on death row, he was murdered by the state of California by way of lethal injection. During the last 25 years of his life Tookie did not wither or crumble under the concrete that held him in captivity. Tookie did not allow the negative environment to influence him instead he stayed positive and changed his life for the better even with the knowledge that his life would end in prison. He preached peace, so much so, that he was visited by Willie Mandela and even won the Nobel Peace Prize while on death row. For this honor him and the principle he stood on: Fortitude.

## 13: Ricky Donnell "Freeway Rick" Ross – Prophet of Principle.

Ricky Donnell "Freeway Rick" Ross is a black man born on January 26th, 1960 to Annie Mae Ross and Sonny Ross in Tyler, Texas. Rick Ross moved to South Central as a boy, where he learned how to play tennis. He was good enough to get a college scholarship to play but failed to do so because he was illiterate. So he entered a community college where eventually he met an upholstery teacher who offered him cocaine to sell. As his operation grew he outgrew supplier after supplier until he eventually was in contact with a Nicaraguan exile who was a supplier. Rick Ross began to get his kilos so cheap that he began to purchase tons, maximizing his profit to where he was making 300 million a year by 1980. As his proceeds continued to grow he began to invest his money especially in real estate which is how he came to earn his name, Freeway Rick. Rick Ross began purchasing properties along "Harbor Freeway" in Los Angeles. His empire expanded over

42 cities by the time he was 25. In 1996 Rick Ross was convicted of "conspiracy to illegally traffic cocaine" and sentenced to life in prison. Earlier in his life (1988) Rick Ross had learned to read while in prison on a pervious case. So after he was convicted and sentenced to life he began to study in the prison law library searching for ways to overturn his conviction. Eventually he found a legal loophole where the courts had erroneously applied the three strikes law. Rick Ross then had his sentence commuted to twenty years by the federal courts of appeal. He was released from prison in 2009. In 2010 he filed a lawsuit against the rapper "Rick Ross" for copyrights infringement for profiting off his likeness. Upon his release he continued to hustle but in a legal way, engaging in business ventures, such as lectures, book sales and a cannabis shop. In 2015 he was arrested on suspicion of possessing cash related to the sale of illegal drugs when police discovered a hundred thousand dollars in his car during a traffic stop. The charges were ultimately dropped because the money was legitimate. Throughout Rick Ross' entire life he strived to do better than the business he was in by trying to go straight to invest into legitimate ventures. Even after 13 years in prison he kept that same mindset and came home touching seven figures by legitimate means. For that honor him and the principle he stands on: motivation.

## 14: Larry Hoover – Prophet of Principle

Larry Hoover is a black man born on November 30th, 1950 in Jackson, Mississippi. Larry Hoover's legacy begins when he is convicted of ordering the murder of a 19 year old man named William "Pooky" Young over stealing drugs and money from his gang "The Gangster Disciples". In 1973, him and his co-defendant who was named as the shooter was sentenced to 150-200 years in prison. While in prison Larry Hoover helped orchestrate the merger of the "Gangster Disciples Nation" and the "Black Disciples Nation" to "Black Gangster Disciples Nation" along with David "King David" Barksdale. In 1974 when King David died, Larry Hoover took over the reins of the organization. While under his leadership they thrived in the drug business and expanded all over the United States. In 1989 after a dispute that led to several murders, the merger broke up and left Larry Hoover leading the "Gangster Disciples" and the "Black Disciples" going their own way. In 1995, Larry Hoover was indicted by the federal government for drug conspiracy, extortion, and continuing to engage in a criminal enterprise while incarcerated at Dixie Correctional Center. In 1997, Larry Hoover and Several other cohorts were found guilty and given life sentences. Larry Hoover is currently serving time in "ADX" located in Florence, Colorado. Urban culture and celebrities alike have been taken various and numerous actions to secure his release. During his almost 50 years of incarceration Larry Hoover has presented himself with courage and dignity. Never has he betrayed anybody for a lower sentence, even refusing offers from the federal government to cooperate for a reduced sentence. He continues to stand on his belief system and looking to educate black youth. For this honor him and the principle he stand on: Dignity.

## 15: Jose Beunvaventura Durruti Demange — Prophet of Principle

---

Durruti was a Spanish man born on July 14th, 1896 to Anastasia Dumange and Santiago Durruti in Leon, Spain. At age 14, Durruti left school to become a railway mechanic in the railway yard in Leon. At the age of 18 he joined the same political group his father was in "Socialist Union General de Trabajadones". Durruti took an active part of the strike in August 1907 called by the group, when the government overturned an agreement between the union and employers. The government sent the Spanish army to end the strike and they did so brutally, killing 70 people in the process. After this Durruti fled to France where he was introduced to Anarchists. After three years over there he returned to Spain in 1920 and formed the paramilitary group, los Justicieros (the Avengers). A year later he and his cohorts tried to assassinate the King Alfonso XIII, unsuccessfully. Durruti then went to Madrid to help foment rebellion, organizing and establishing the "los Solidarious" (the Solidarity) In the following years. In 1923 the group was implicated in the assassination of a cardinal as reprisal for the death of an anarchist. Durruti became more passionate about the anarchist movement and began to organize attacks on military barracks in Barcelona and near France. He also began to travel to Cuba, Chile and Argentina to carry out bank robberies in order to finance his coalition. In the 1930's, Durrutis character started to strengthen due to the losses he began to suffer. Such as two of his brothers being murdered while participating in union strikes and attacks. After losing a comrade in the battle of "Atarazanas Barracks" Durruti led over three thousand armed anarchists throughout the streets of Barcelona and Zaragoza. He went on to capture many cities throughout this march by engaging in bloody battles with the Spanish army. Durruti was shot and killed by friendly fire while in a battle located inside Madrid in November, 1936. A few hours after Durruti's death, his troops killed 52 policemen who were captured as reprisal. Even in death Durruti continues to be celebrated as a hero for his leadership values and valor. He began to engage in military battles in his youth with no formal training rising to the top of the ranks by letting his experience guide him to leadership by way of wisdom. For this honor him and the principle he stood on: Empiricism.

## 16: Demetrius Edwards "Big Meech" Flenory – Prophet of Principle

Big Meech is a black man born on June 21, 1968 in Detroit, Michigan. Big Meech began his earlier career of selling drugs when he started to sell $50 bags of cocaine in high school in the late 1980's. After a brief prison stint in the nineties Big Meech began to rise to the top of the underworld with his brother "Southwest T", after securing a Mexican Cartel plug. Shortly after securing this connection, he and his brother began to move hundreds of kilo's throughout the United States. Including but not limited to: Alabama, California, Georgia, Florida, Michigan, Kentucky, Louisiana, Mississippi, Missouri, North Carolina, Ohio and Tennessee. His network entailed bringing tons of cocaine through California from Mexico and having it transported to Atlanta to be placed in stash and distribution houses. In an attempt to make the money seem legit, Big Meech founded the record label "BMF ENT". Giving a name to his U.S. based drug cartel, "The Black Mafia Family." He promoted his artist through the company as well as several other major artists, including young Jeezy. At BMF's height they were selling up to 150 kilos a week. Approximately three million dollars' worth of drugs. In 2005 Big Meech along with other BMF members were indicted for a sleuth of charges including, continuing a criminal enterprise and racketeering. As the indictment started to fall, more and more BMF members began to fold and cooperate with the federal government for leniency. Mistakenly the prosecution thought Big Meech was made of the same stuff and offered him twenty years in return for his testimony. Big Meech declined and was sentenced to thirty years in 2008. While living in prison it is reported that Big Meech has stuck to the script after all his years of hustling. Big Meech has never compromised his morals and values. He took responsibility for himself and only himself by adhering to secrecy while others took an easier road. For this honor him and the principle he stands on: integrity.

## 17: George Jackson — Prophet of Principle

George Jackson was a black man born September 23, 1941 in Chicago, Illinois. He was born at the end of the great depression. So needless to say he grew up in extreme poverty. Growing up as an adolescent, George continuously engaged in mischief. Sometimes even having contact with the law. In 1956, him and his father moved to Los Angeles where his run in's with the law started to become more serious and more frequent. At the age of 15, he was shot six times by a police officer for breaking into a department store. By the time he was 18 he was given a one to life sentence for the robbery of a gas station for seventy dollars. While in prison, he began to educate himself on socioeconomics and politics. He began to go through a transformation from the criminal mind to radicalization. AT the time, he was incarcerated in one of the most deadly prisons in America, San Quentin. Racism and race wars were extremely common in this prison.

George Jackson credited this for his reason of radicalization into a revolutionary. He is largely recognized by the underworld as one of the founder of the "Black Guerilla Family". A prison gang centered around black education and black protection. George became a national figure when he and two others (John Clutchette and Fleeta Drumgo) were accused of murdering a prison guard for retaliation of a black prisoner being murdered by guards in a prison riot. At this time he became connected with the prophet Angela Davis as she helped him in his legal defense and grassroots movement to secure his freedom. They began a romantic relationship soon after meeting. Together they pushed his book "Soledad Brothers" around the country. While Angela Davis was incarcerated, waiting to stand trial for allegedly aiding his brother Johnathon in a failed jail break, George Jackson was assassinated by prison guards. He was shot in the head by a guard in the gun tower. The prison concocted many stories to justify his homicide, all as baseless as the first. During his lifetime George went from criminal to revolutionary by educating himself. From behind the walls, he helped create a movement that changed the dynamics of blacks in prison. He became a writer and a poet. A martyr for the cause of revolution by way of his pen and his efforts. For this honor him and the principle he stood one: education.

www.ingramcontent.com/pod-product-compliance
Lightning Source LLC
Chambersburg PA
CBHW071909070526
44583CB00016B/1906